SALAMANDERS

John Woodward

Grolier
an imprint of
SCHOLASTIC
www.scholastic.com/librarypublishing

Published 2008 by Grolier
An imprint of Scholastic Library Publishing
Old Sherman Turnpike, Danbury,
Connecticut 06816

For The Brown Reference Group plc
Project Editor: Jolyon Goddard
Copy-editors: Lesley Ellis, Lisa Hughes,
    Wendy Horobin
Picture Researcher: Clare Newman
Designers: Jeni Child, Lynne Ross,
    Sarah Williams
Managing Editor: Bridget Giles

Volume ISBN-13: 978-0-7172-6261-8
Volume ISBN-10: 0-7172-6261-8

**Library of Congress
Cataloging-in-Publication Data**

Nature's children. Set 2.
    p. cm.
Includes bibliographical references and
index.
ISBN-13: 978-0-7172-8081-0
ISBN-10: 0-7172-8081-0
1. Animals--Encyclopedias, Juvenile. I.
Grolier (Firm)
QL49.N383 2007
590--dc22
                2007026928

Printed and bound in China

PICTURE CREDITS

Front Cover: **Shutterstock**: Anita Huszti

Back Cover: **Nature PL**: Ingo Arndt, Todd
Pusser, Jose B. Ruis; **NHPA**: Karl Switak

Ardea: Mary Clay 10; **Nature PL**: Jane
Burton 46, Philippe Clement 5, 45, Fabio
Liverani 9, 14, 38, Barry Mansell 4, 18, 42,
Todd Pusser 6, 29, Jose B. Ruiz 22, Doug
Wechsler 41; **NHPA**: Robert Erwin 13, Eric
Soder 33; **Photolibrary.com**: Marty
Cordano 30, David M. Dennis 21, 37, Breck P.
Kent 34; **Shutterstock**: Stephen Bonk 17,
Carsten Reisinger 26–27; **Still Pictures**: R.
Andrew Odum 2–3.

Contents

FACT FILE: Salamanders

Class	Amphibians (Amphibia)
Order	Caudates (Caudata)
Families	10 families worldwide
Genera	More than 35 worldwide
Species	At least 410 worldwide
World distribution	Mainly the cooler parts of North America, Europe, and Asia, but some live in tropical Central America and South America
Habitat	Mainly moist, shady woods, with water for breeding; some always live in water
Distinctive physical characteristics	Long body and tail, with four or sometimes just two short legs; smooth, moist skin; many are brightly colored
Habits	Active mainly at night, and only in warmer months; many return to the water to breed in spring
Diet	Insects, spiders, snails, slugs, and worms

Introduction

The word *salamander* means "fire lizard" in Greek. People used to see salamanders crawling out of logs that had been thrown on the fire. The animals were trying to escape, but their observers thought they were able to live in the fire.

Salamanders come in all sizes and colors. Some don't have any lungs and others can lose and regrow their tail. These unique creatures thrive in ponds, rivers, lakes, streams, rain forests, and grasslands. In fact, salamanders can be found on every continent except Antarctica.

European salamanders bask on a rock.

A mud salamander
rests on some lichen.

Frogs With Tails

A typical salamander looks somewhat like a lizard, with a long body, short legs, and a long tail. But instead of the dry scaly skin of a lizard, a salamander has soft, moist skin like a frog. Salamanders are the same type of animals as frogs. They are both **amphibians**. Lizards, like snakes, are reptiles.

Amphibians are animals that spend part of their life in the water and part on land. When they are on land, amphibians have to stay in damp or dark places. Amphibians lose moisture through their skin. They would dry out if they stayed in the sun for too long. Most amphibians also have to lay their eggs in the water.

Salamanders, however, break many rules that govern most other amphibians. Some of these creatures live in the water, while others stay on land. Still others do both. A few salamanders even live in caves, while others climb trees!

Land and Water

Aquatic, or water-living, salamanders and **newts** live in rivers, lakes, ponds, creeks, swamps, and even in streams that flow through underground caves. Salamander species that live on land usually make their home under rocks or rotting logs. It is shady and damp in those places, and the animals are not likely to dry out there.

Most salamanders live in cooler parts of the world, such as North America and northern Asia. But new species are being discovered all the time in the tropical forests of Central and South America. These tropical rain forest salamanders are expert climbers. They spend their life among the wet leaves high up in trees.

A cave salamander makes its way across damp rocks.

A tiger salamander—a type of mole salamander—eats a juicy earthworm.

Shiny Beauties

Some of the most attractive salamanders are the colorful mole salamanders, which live only in North America. They get their name from the way they burrow like moles.

Many mole salamanders are beautiful, with shiny black or brown skin and vividly colored spots or stripes. They often look plump and well fed. They have vertical creases on their sides that allow them to wriggle around easily.

Mole salamanders are not often seen. But in spring they make overland treks to ponds, where they lay their eggs. That is when these amphibians are most likely to be seen—although they usually travel by night to avoid drying out on a sunny day.

Wrinkly Giants

Most salamanders are small, fairly attractive animals that measure less than 6 inches (15 cm) long. But some are ugly monsters! The three species of giant salamanders live in rivers in Japan, China, and North America. The largest is the Japanese giant salamander. It can grow to 60 inches (150 cm) long and weigh up to 75 pounds (34 kg)! The American hellbender is much smaller, growing to around 28 inches (70 cm). But that is still a giant compared with most other salamanders.

These giants have tiny eyes and wrinkly skin, which makes them look very old. Some of them might actually be old—they can live for at least 50 years. Giant salamanders never leave the water and usually spend their days hidden beneath rocks. They creep out at night to feed on other animals, which often include smaller salamanders!

This hellbender
salamander
lives in Utah.

This crested
newt has a large
fin on its tail.

Newt Relatives

Salamanders have some close relatives called newts. The main difference between newts and salamanders is the way in which they live. Most adult salamanders live either in water or on land—although many land-living salamanders lay their eggs in water.

By contrast, most newts spend around half the year on land and half in the water. Instead of just visiting the water to lay eggs, newts stay there all summer. Some newts even grow fins on their tail and develop webbed feet, which help them swim better!

Newts are so closely related to salamanders that they belong to one of the 10 salamander families. In fact, newts are actually types of salamanders.

Newts and Efts

When newts are living in water, they have sleek, shiny skin, just as typical salamanders do. But when they are living on land, they often look quite different. They have rough, leathery skin. During the land-dwelling stage of their life, they are called **efts** rather than newts.

One of the best-known North American newts is the red-spotted newt of the eastern United States. The young red-spotted newt lives the first part of its life in water. When it leaves the water to live on land it turns into a dark orange, red-spotted form called a red eft. This animal lives on land for two or three years, but then changes again. Its skin smooths out and changes color, turning olive green, although it still has red spots. Meanwhile, its tail turns into a flattened swimming fin. In this form, the red-spotted newt makes its way back to the water to **breed** as an adult.

A red-spotted
newt crawls across
a tree stump.

A marbled
salamander
has moist black-
and-white skin.

18

Breathable Skin

If salamanders are not careful, they can lose too much body moisture through their skin and die. But there is a good reason why a salamander's skin allows water and even air in and out of its body. Since the skin takes in and lets out water and air, the salamander doesn't have to drink or breathe much. That is particularly useful underwater. Like air, most water contains the **oxygen** that animals need. A salamander can **absorb** this oxygen through its skin. As a result, it doesn't have to go to the water's surface to breathe air so often.

When a salamander is on land, it can also absorb oxygen through its skin—provided the skin always has a thin covering of water. This water is kept in place by a slippery layer of **mucus**, or sticky slime, which is why most salamanders look so wet and shiny.

Look, No Lungs

Some salamanders do not really breathe at all, even though they live mainly on land. They cannot breathe because they do not have any lungs. Not surprisingly, these salamanders are called "lungless salamanders."

Lungless salamanders form the largest family of salamanders in the world. These salamanders rely on their moist skin to absorb oxygen from the air. But if a lungless salamander needs extra oxygen, it gets it by gaping its mouth open. The skin inside its mouth is very thin and allows oxygen to pass into its blood. The salamander pumps air in and out of its mouth using its throat. That also helps it test the air for scents that could lead it to food.

Lungless salamanders must stay moist otherwise they cannot absorb oxygen through their skin. Therefore, they must live in dark, damp places.

The spotted dusky
salamander is
a lungless
salamander.

A sharp-ribbed salamander has shed part of its skin.

New Skin

As a salamander grows, its outer skin stretches. But eventually it cannot stretch any more and needs to be replaced. In some species, such as thicker-skinned newts, the skin peels off whole. The animal has to wriggle a lot to get it off. The old skin eventually slips off its tail to reveal a brand-new skin that has grown underneath it. Newts often eat the old skin rather than waste it. The thinner skins of many other salamanders come off in bits and pieces, so they do not get a chance to eat them.

Poisonous Defenses

All sorts of animals try to attack and eat salamanders. These **predators** include snakes, birds, shrews, fish, frogs, and even large beetles and spiders. Luckily, salamanders have ways of defending themselves that can scare off their enemies for good.

Many salamanders produce poisons that squirt through holes in their skin when they are frightened. The poisons make them taste horrible, and they can be deadly to some animals. The European fire salamander can even spray its poison through the air, aiming it accurately for 10 feet (3 m) or more! If the spray gets in a person's eyes, it causes a burning pain and can even make them blind for a short while!

These poisonous salamanders are often brightly colored. These colorings remind the salamander's predators of its dangerous nature. Salamanders often show off these colors in a special defensive **display**. Their enemies soon learn to avoid them!

A Trick of the Tail

When some types of salamanders get into
serious trouble, they can escape by making
their tail break off! The animal raises its tail
high in the air and waves it about. Then the tail
suddenly snaps off, falls to the ground, and
keeps on wriggling and squirming by itself!
Enemies, such as birds, find this event so
fascinating that they keep watching the tail—
and do not notice its owner creeping away to
hide! Often, the tail is covered with poison that
has oozed from the skin. The predator then gets
a second surprise when it tries to eat the tail—
which tastes horrible.

Meanwhile, the salamander has no tail. But
that is not a problem for long because it grows
a new one. It can even grow a new leg if it loses
one in a fight. It takes a few months for a
salamander to regrow a lost leg or tail.

This salamander's colorful skin warns predators that it is poisonous to eat.

Amphiumas

Some of the strangest salamanders are the three species of amphiumas (AM-FEE-OO-MAZ) that live in the swamps of the southeastern United States. At first glance, they look just like eels. They have a long slender body and shiny slippery skin. They do have legs but they are so small that they are easy to miss, and they are probably almost useless. Amphiumas spend nearly all of their time in water, although they might creep out onto land during rainstorms.

The largest of these unusual creatures is the three-toed amphiuma, which can grow to more than 36 inches (90 cm) long. The two-toed and one-toed amphiumas are much smaller.

A two-toed amphiuma rests in shallow water.

This tiger salamander's teeth are too small to kill a fat worm, so it will swallow its prey alive.

Eaten Alive

Salamanders eat other small animals. They feed on anything they can catch and swallow. Their food includes caterpillars, beetles, worms, slugs, and snails. Salamanders that live in water also eat small fish, crayfish, freshwater shrimps, and sometimes other, smaller salamanders.

A few species have an extendible, sticky tongue. They can shoot it forward in a split second to capture animals crawling over nearby leaves or rocks. But most salamanders seize their prey in their jaws, using their small teeth to grip it and stop it from escaping. Salamander teeth are too small to kill their victims, however. The salamanders swallow their prey whole and alive!

Winter Sleep

Most salamanders live in places that have cold
winters. Unlike people, a salamander cannot
keep itself warm in winter. Its body temperature
is always the same as its surroundings. As the
weather gets colder, a salamander's body gets
colder, too. That slows it down. Eventually,
it can barely move at all, so it has to find
somewhere to hide until spring.

Most salamanders bury themselves deep in
the ground, in holes among tree roots, or inside
rotting logs. The earth or timber protects them
from the worst of the cold and stops them from
freezing. They fall into a deep sleep called
hibernation. During this time they use so little
energy that they do not have to eat at all for
months. Eventually, warmer weather wakes
them up. The salamanders dig their way to the
surface and start hunting again.

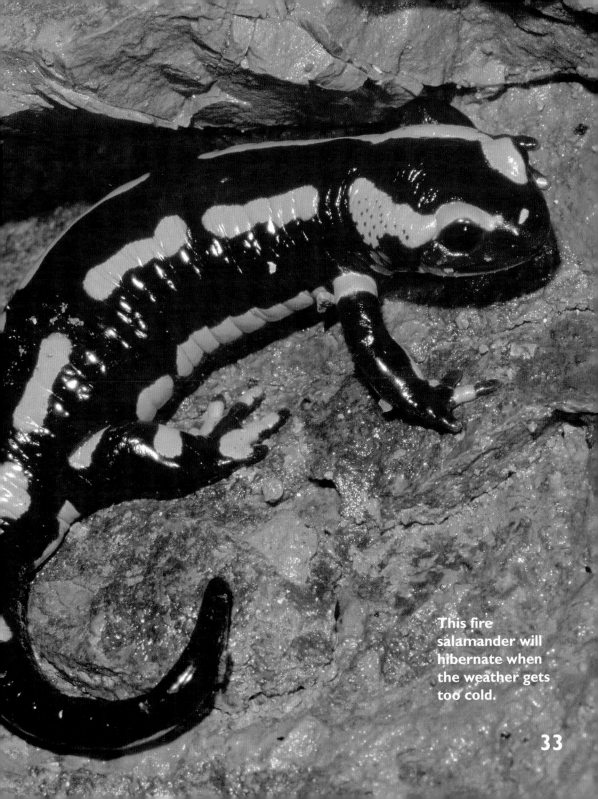

This fire salamander will hibernate when the weather gets too cold.

The greater siren salamander has just one pair of small legs at the front of its body.

Summer Retreat

Some salamanders have difficulty surviving
hot, dry summers, including siren salamanders.
These salamanders are long eel-like animals,
somewhat like amphiumas. Siren salamanders
have just one pair of legs, positioned at the
front of their body. These salamanders live
underwater in shallow ponds and marshes
in the southern United States and Mexico. In
dry summers, their pools can dry up. Since
these salamanders do not have proper legs,
they cannot escape to find another home.

Instead, they burrow into the drying mud
of pond beds and produce a mass of sticky
slime, called mucus. This slime hardens to
form a protective case, or **cocoon**, which keeps
the salamander safe and healthy. The animal
can survive like this for around two months or
more, until the rain falls and its pool fills up
once again.

Incredible Journey

Soon after emerging from hibernation, salamanders are ready to breed. Some are able to lay their eggs on land, in wet places such as rotting logs. But most salamanders that live on land have to lay their eggs in water, just as frogs do. In early spring, the salamanders begin making their way to suitable pools. They often head for the ponds in which they were born.

No one knows exactly how salamanders find their way to these breeding ponds. But tests have shown that some species use the position of the Sun. They might also direct themselves by using Earth's **magnetic field**, which is an invisible forcefield between the north and south poles.

Either way, salamanders seem to have an internal "map" that guides them on journeys of 9 miles (15 km) or more! That is an incredible distance for animals with such short legs.

A four-toed salamander has laid a lot of eggs.

During the breeding season, the male alpine newt has a bright crest and colorful body.

Courting Couples

Salamanders breed in all kinds of ways. When American spotted salamanders travel to their breeding ponds, they all arrive at the same time. They mate, lay their eggs, and leave, all within a few days. Other species, such as giant salamanders, never leave the water. On the other hand, some species, such as lungless woodland salamanders, never go near water.

Whether they breed on land or in the water, most male salamanders and newts use special **courtship** displays to impress females. Each species has its own dance routine, which often involves clinging to the female. Some male European newts even grow a large, colorful crest. That makes them more attractive to the females. Eventually, the salamanders mate, and the female is then able to lay her eggs.

Salamander Eggs

Nearly all salamanders hatch from eggs. These eggs are laid in water or in moist places on land. Salamanders that lay their eggs in water produce up to 500 eggs at a time. But many of these eggs are likely to be eaten by fish or other animals. Salamanders that lay their eggs on land usually produce between 20 and 30 eggs. Salamanders sometimes guard their eggs until they hatch.

The eggs look like dark blobs surrounded by clear gel—similar to frog spawn. The gel forms a protective covering. But the eggs do not have waterproof shells like those of birds or reptiles. That is why the eggs must be laid in damp places or underwater. Otherwise they would soon dry out and die.

These spotted salamander eggs are tinged green because they contain tiny, plantlike living organisms.

Feathery gills stick out on this tiger salamander larva.

Fishy Larvae

Salamander eggs that are laid in water hatch into small, fishlike creatures. They have a long tail and no legs. These animals look similar to frog tadpoles. Each salamander baby is called a **larva**. They have feathery **gills** that help them absorb oxygen from the water. These larvae don't have to come to the surface to breathe air. Many larvae also have a pair of sticklike "balancers" dangling from their head. These structures help the larvae stay upright. The larvae feed on tiny water animals and might even eat one another. Normally, however, the larvae spread out in the water, away from one another. That way they don't often get the chance to feed on one another. Over time, each larva grows a pair of front legs from tiny buds on the lower side of its body. It then grows a pair of back legs. Eventually, the larva begins to look more like an adult salamander.

Changing Shape

Gradually, the baby salamanders go through a dramatic change. As well as growing legs, they develop adult skin. Most larvae lose their feathery gills and grow lungs. The young salamanders will then have to visit the water's surface to breathe. Eventually, most young salamanders stop living in the water altogether and crawl out onto the land. This type of huge change is called **metamorphosis**.

Salamanders that are born on land develop differently. The whole transformation from larva to young salamander happens inside the protective gel of the egg. Eventually, each egg hatches as a miniature salamander—a tiny version of its parents. The females of some land-breeding species keep their eggs inside their body and give birth to fully formed babies.

These European salamanders might look the same, but they have slightly different color patterns.

This salamander, called an axolotl, has gills and lives in water for its entire life.

Feathery Gills

Some salamanders stay in the water for their entire life. They include the mudpuppy, which lives in lakes, rivers, and creeks in northeastern North America. It can grow to 16 inches (40 cm) long and is gray or brown, with dark blue spots. Its most obvious features, however, are the red feathery gills that sprout from its neck. They are red because they are full of blood. The gills absorb oxygen more easily than the animal's skin. That allows the salamander to live in stagnant water that does not contain much oxygen. Mudpuppies that live in less stagnant water have smaller gills.

Similar salamanders called water dogs live in the southeastern United States, and an unusual creamy-white relative called the olm lives in southern Europe. The olm lives in the total darkness of caves and it is completely blind!

Taking Care

Salamanders are an important part of nature. They provide food for other animals and help keep down the numbers of pests, such as slugs and flies. Salamanders eat huge numbers of mosquito larvae, which helps prevent the spread of dangerous diseases, such as malaria and West Nile virus infection.

It is important to protect salamanders and their habitat. People can do that in many ways. If someone finds a salamander resting under a rock, he or she should carefully place the rock back over the salamander. Otherwise it might become too dry in the sun. On a larger scale, people can protect salamanders by making sure that the animals have places to live on land and by not draining or poisoning the pools in which these amazing amphibians live and breed.

Words to Know

Absorb   Soak something up.

Amphibians   Types of animals that might live both on land and in the water.

Aquatic   Water-living.

Breed   Come together to produce young.

Cocoon   A protective covering for an animal that is inactive.

Courtship   Actions to impress animals of the other sex, so they agree to breed.

Display   A performance that sends a message to another animal.

Efts   The land-living form of a newt.

Energy   The force that keeps an animal alive, which it gets from its food.

Gills	Structures that help an animal "breathe" underwater.
Hibernation	A deep, sleeplike state that lasts all winter.
Larva	The young, water-living stage of a typical salamander's life.
Magnetic field	A force that makes a compass needle point north.
Metamorphosis	A big change in an animal's form that alters its way of life.
Mucus	A sticky substance secreted by a salamander's skin.
Newts	Types of salamanders that live partly on land and partly in water.
Oxygen	A gas that animals need to live.
Predators	Animals that hunt other animals.

Find Out More

Books

McNab, C. *Frogs, Toads, and Salamanders*. Strongsville, Ohio: Gareth Stevens Publishing, 2005.

Stebbins, R. C. *Western Reptiles and Amphibians*. Peterson Field Guides. New York, New York: Houghton Mifflin, 2003.

Web sites

Salamander
www.enchantedlearning.com/subjects/amphibians/Salamander printout.shtml
Includes illustrated life-cycle diagram.

San Diego Zoo
www.sandiegozoo.org/animalbytes/t-salamander.html
Facts about salamanders and newts.

Index